T0146730

It's Halftime America

It's Halftime America

*"Use "Football Basics" to Reshape America
and Its Politics . . . . A Light History of Football,
Politics and the USA.*

Joseph L. Ernstes

Rev. date: 06/23/2016

To order additional copies of this book, contact:
Xlibris
1-888-795-4274
www.Xlibris.com
Orders@Xlibris.com
740054

As an undersized high school football player, I would not have survived if not for the help and encouragement of my teammates. Thanks to Blasdel, Darby, Harmon,Hellmich, Riedeman, Tucker, Wilson and many others, for watching my back.

CONTENTS

INTRODUCTION

One of my first memories of football was the old AFL, the American Football League, that upstart organization that dared to challenge the status quo, the NFL.

What stood out to me the most at a young age of 9 or 10, was the yard line markers. In the AFL you had markers every 5 yards, so when you looked at the fieled you saw the 5, the 10, the 15, the 20 and so on. I thought that was so cool.

An odd memory I guess, but a memory nonetheless.

I also came to enjoy some very colorful personalities in the AFL, with names that bounced off your tongue.

There was the announcer Al DeRogatis, players like Nick Buonicanti, Jan Stenerud, Cookie Gilchrist and many others. Then there was that really old guy, George Blanda, my god, that guy was 40! And he was still winning football games both with his arm and his leg.

His team Oakland, beat Kansas City in a playoff game in the late 60's, that I remember watching on a black and white set in my parent's basement. It was one of the greatest games ever.

Even though I was a scrawny, slow, Midwestern kid, I fell in love with the battles, the contact and the struggles of the game. It taught me that Football was a metaphor for life. Fight, battle, get knocked down, get back up and try again.

My neighbor Tim, two years older, toughened us up by inflicting numerous tackles on me and my brothers in the name of Ray Nitscke, the feared Green Bay Packers middle line backer of the 60's.

At 4'10 and 85 lbs, I was probably the smallest center in the history of middle school football. But I didn't care. Football was fun.

The fortunes of life are like the fortunes of a football team. There are struggles, setbacks, wins, losses, and comebacks in both. Everyone contributes, everyone pulls their own weight and as a team you move forward.

The same can be said for the struggles we face as a country. After over 200 years of struggles, World Wars, depressions, recessions, we have persevered. The struggles and comebacks of this great country will continue, and the success of this country will continue,

In Football, when a team has problems, the answer is not to reverse course or make rash changes, just because others have cried out for such moves.

The answer is to get back to basics, pull together and move ahead once more. So it is with this great country.

Let's get back to basics America.

I'm here to talk about Football, America and the future direction of this country. These are random topics but yet related in how they weave a story we can all understand.

We'll look at some of football's early leaders, how did they handle adversity?

How did America's early leaders handle the trials and tribulations of a new, growing nation? How does the USA, stay on track?

What can we learn from football to apply to rejuvenating this country?

Let's find out.

We are at a crossroads here in America or as I like to think of it, we are at halftime of a very big football game.

We all know what halftime is about, but here, I am not talking about going to the restroom, chasing down another hot dog or grabbing another beer.

Those all have their rightful place.

I'm talking about being "in" the locker room, getting yelled at by the head coach, being challenged to reach down deep, to come up with a better second half performance.
I'm talking about "Gut Check" time.

"Anyone who thinks we can't come back shouldn't go out there again". The late Coach Jerry Schmidt to his team (Hobart) during the halftime with Hobart trailing Cornell 7-2 in 1978.
Hobart briefly took a 11-10 lead in the 4th Qtr, but fell 13-11.

Many of you have played football at one time or another in your lives, or you have participated in other teams sports
You have been in the locker room at halftime and know how it feels, when your coach is asking you to dig deep, to get back to basics, so you can overcome a poor first half performance.
Well, that is what's facing us today in this country.
We are in the locker room hoping to overcome a really BAD first half, (really a BAD 7-8 years is more like it)

So what does football have to do with righting the floundering economic ship called the USS United States of America.

It has a lot to do with it.

The early football players in this nation were drawn to the battle, or the contest itself. Yes, winning was important, but competing, testing your mettle, was the main draw. Could we as a team, stand together, and through the contribution of the individual team members, pull together as one unit to build something, to succeed. Going forward can we as a team adjust, to meet challenges, and thwart adversity?
Seems like a natural correlation then between football and this country. Building and maintaining a football team, or a country, takes

hard work and the contributions of all. The question now, at this juncture in our country's history, is will we pull together to create continued success?

When the game is on the line, you go back to the basics, you return to the core.

It's the basics of your team, the fundamentals, the way you play, the hard work, the blocking and tackling. This is what you go back to doing.

Basics, in other words the system, the exercises, the drills, the fundamentals, that got you to this point.

What works, what got us here?

Is it time for a new offense, do we change our playbook at halftime because it is considered passé, or old fashioned? Do we change because of the outcries, the boo's, or because of what another team may be doing?

No, in the quaint parlance of the Midwestern farm girl, at the local hoedown on Saturday night,

"You dance with the one that brung ya"

ROOTS OF AMERICAN FOOTBALL

Until the early 20th Century, in football games, the ball had to be "touched down" in the end zone. (Hence the term we use today for a score). Which of course meant if an offensive player got through, carrying the ball, a defensive player could, literally, hold him up and toss him back out and there was NO SCORE.

For a long time, also, a score was only 5 points.

Whaaatt? You mean you didn't automatically get 6 points? All that hard work to move the ball down the field and to even cross the plane into the end zone and you possibly get nothing? Why or who would play such a game?

Some say that the rising popularity of football in America had naturally followed the diminishing Indian Wars. It was as though America, at a loss as to what to do at the end of the Indian wars, hit on football as an answer for this want of violence.

Harvard, Princeton, Yale and Columbia, formed the Intercollegiate Football Association on Nov 22, 1876. This followed by just 4 months the annihilation of General George Custer and his troops at the Little Big Horn. By the 1890's the nation was intensely interested in the sport as a proving ground for young males and as a sort of a remedy to the gentrification of the times.

At schools across the country young men, very lightly padded in the scant uniforms of the day, slammed into each other, spilling blood. New massive stadiums went up so that spectators could watch this new manly contest. Some say this popularity soothed a nations fears that its' young men would be growing up too soft. Football was blossoming, and would become a major part in the 1920's of what was titled, "The Golden Age of Sports", led by such royalty as Babe Ruth of the New York Yankees, Red Grange of the "Fighting Illini" at the University of Illinois, and Jack Dempsey in the boxing ring. Sports were becoming a nationwide fascination.

Preoccupied with this new sport, in the early part of the 20th century were the Cadets at West Point Military Academy and later a small little known Indian school in PA, called Carlisle.

Their paths would cross in battle, in the early part of the century.

It would be a battle never forgotten.

HOW LONG HAVE WE
BEEN AROUND?

The Constitution was written and adopted back in 1789, with the more famous date of July 4th 1776, which is the date the Declaration of Independence was drawn up.

Since the adoption of the Constitution by the original states, there have been many challenges to it. Our forefathers, anticipating this might happen put in a series of checks and balances to be administered by the three branches of government, the Legislative, Executive and Judicial branches, so that no one area of government could extend it's reach past certain boundaries.

Over the years, we have seen these many challenges, and some of these have changed the way we look at things.

During the great depression, President Franklin Roosevelt developed many government led programs to put people to work. These many programs were challenged by some, who felt his reach had extended too far, that these were unconstitutional. Did these programs work?

Well, in the short run they did, by providing a paycheck for families, so that they could put food on the table, but they did not turn into the economic driver that some boasted they would. The old saying, "Give a man a fish you feed him for a day, teach a man to fish, you feed him for a lifetime", seems to apply here.

The nation learned then, as most of us know, that the Government is not the driver of the US economy, but you would get an argument from the current Obama administration on that. As he is now famously quoted as telling American businesses and entrepreneurs,

"You didn't build that"

His feeling is that capitalism is "Not Fair," that businesses are built and grow unfairly by exploiting the workers. Well, one of the great rights we enjoy in this country is that we are not confined to a particular class. We do not have to remain just a worker, if we aspire to greater heights. We can found and build companies and we can employ workers through these companies.

The list of large companies started by an individual with nothing but an idea is extremely long and always growing.

We have a choice. Government running of the economy takes away this choice. Still many politicians feel that the direction of America should be toward a more socialist path.

George Santayana's aphorism comes to mind:

"Those who cannot remember the past are condemned to repeat it," should serve as a sober reminder that every generation is responsible for handing down the knowledge and wisdom attained by previous generations.

Those who study the revisionist-plundered history lessons showing up in some of the "government schools" today, may be surprised to learn

America already experimented with socialism. Out of that failed experiment emerged our free-market, capitalist economic system.

AMERICA, THE EARLY DAYS

America's first experiment with socialism wasn't Lyndon Johnson's Great Society, nor was it Franklin Roosevelt's New Deal—although both made sweeping changes to the nation's underlying government structure and entrapped America in the bureaucratic quagmire of collectivism. No, America's very first experiment with redistribution of wealth occurred before America was officially a nation.

In 1620, the Puritan Pilgrims arrived in the "desolate wilderness" of Plymouth, Massachusetts. (And you thought Cleveland was bad in the winter.)

Seeking escape from religious persecution in Europe, the Puritans risked their lives crossing the Atlantic to establish a new colony in the unknown wilderness of America. The Pilgrims decided that their new community would practice collectivism, which is an early name for socialism. All labor was communal fro both men and women. The men were busy raising crops for all families, and women handled domestic chores for their family and their neighbors.

The Pilgrims' Governor, William Bradford, later described the folly, "the practice of collectivism," or as it is know today "socialism."

"The experience that was had in this common course and condition, tried sundry years, and that amongst godly and sober men, may well evince the vanity of that conceit of Plato's and other ancients applauded by some of later times; that the taking away of property and bringing in community into a commonwealth would make them happy and flourishing; as if they were wiser than God.

(Wow, the governor spoke like a real governor, a far cry from the the collective dribble we get from some of today's politicians.) Going on he said,

"For this collectivist community was found to breed much confusion and discontent, and retard much employment that would have been to their benefit and comfort.

The young men, that were most able and fit for labor and service, complained that why should they spend their time and strength to work for other men's wives and children without any benefit. The strong had no more in division of food and clothes than the weak and the weak, unable to do a quarter the strong could; this was thought injustice. The aged and graver men, to be ranked and equalized in labor output, thought it some indignity and disrespect unto them.

And for men's wives to be commanded to do service for other men, as dressing their meat, washing their clothes, etc., they deemed it a kind of slavery, the husbands didn't care for it much either.

The Pilgrims, a pious and decent people, discovered that even the best of men cannot thrive under socialism's incentive-crushing system. This experiment with socialism—probably its best chance for success amongst such selfless, righteous people—failed miserably. The Puritans discovered that government cannot deny man's inherent desire to work hard to provide for his own family and be rewarded when his labor exceeds his neighbor's.

Having learned a valuable lesson about human nature, the Pilgrims chose to establish a new economic system that encouraged and rewarded personal initiative.

Instead of a collectivist labor force, each family was given a plot of land on which to grow their own crops. Soon, each family was pulling its own weight. In fact, the harvest was so bountiful that the Pilgrims were able to trade with local Indians, (not the Cleveland Indians) and the colony prospered. Bradford reflected on the success of this capitalist approach to private labor:

"They had very good success, for it made all hands very industrious, so as much more corn was planted than otherwise would have been.

The women now went willingly into the field, and took their little ones with them to set corn"

The Pilgrims learned that by the time the harvest came, that instead of famine, now God gave them plenty, and the faces of things were changed. There was rejoicing in the hearts of many, for which they thanked God. Indeed, their bounty was so great, that they had enough to not only trade among themselves but also with the neighboring Indians in the forest."

Nowadays, the Puritans are sometimes maligned and disparaged by the politically correct crowd for their religious devotion.

Americans should be thankful to these brave souls for not only bringing the concept of religious freedom across the Atlantic, but for surviving America's first experiment with socialism. The misery they experienced under socialism led to the free-market economy later established by their descendents.

The appeal of socialism is that it seems a benevolent form of government, where everyone works to help his fellow citizens. There is nothing wrong in helping our fellow citizens. But, as the Puritans discovered, socialism denies man's innate incentive to work hard, and prosper, for his own family. Capitalism, while not perfect, gives man the incentive he needs to work hard for his family and thereby help his entire community—not by force, but out of true generosity. If America fails to learn from the mistakes of our ancestors, that tried collectivism (socialism), we'll have forgotten the truth of Albert Einstein's famous aphorism:

"Insanity: doing the same thing over and over again and expecting different results."

Many other nations around the world have pursued this line of thinking and they have ended up with a brand of socialism that has resulted in high unemployment, high government dependence, and a low standing in the world. Look at the suffering today in many oil rich South American countries, and many of the old guard nations of Europe.

Is that what we want for America?

Well the short answer is no.

The more involved answer is Hell, NO!

DOES BIG GOVERNMENT WORK?

President Obama follows the thinking of noted economist John Maynard Keynes, which is essentially that full employment could be maintained only with the help government spending. All growth in a country flows from the government, rather from the efforts of the private sector. One question here, Mr. Keynes, where does the government obtain its resources? The answer is that government obtains its resources through taxation of us, from us, from the private sector. A Nation cannot continue to exist, much less flourish in this manner. You can't continue to take from the efforts of others to serve those not contributing.

A football team cannot exist and succeed in this manner. Can you imagine what happens when only one half or two thirds of the team does its job?

What if the tackles decided they just didn't want to block, as the guards were doing, or the only blocks they threw were "look out" blocks, as my high school football coach, Coach Steve House, used to call them, (Hey look out!)

What if the wide receivers decided not to run their routes because they knew the QB would probably hand off to the running back anyway?

How much success would that team have?

Well, very little, because success follows everyone pulling their own weight and doing their job. In the mindset of many this isn't necessary and many also feel that they fruits of others labors should be shared.

The Federal government, often in an effort to maintain its voting base, continues to make it easy for people not to pull their own weight. Why go out and look for a job when you can sit at home collecting food stamps and drawing unemployment?

What happened to pride in oneself?

Still the government tells us that Big Government will take care of them.

Well how well has that worked these past 7 -8 years?

What sets the United States apart from other countries is this lack of socialism, which we call market capitalism. Give people a chance to succeed and they will flock to this country. This is also referred to as American Exceptionalism.

Now many people confuse this term with a boast that we as Americans are better than people of other nations, and that is not the case. What this means is there is an exceptional opportunity available in this country that is found no where else in the world,

Compare this with the many countries that are ruled by monarchs, or exist in some sort of socialist society.

"Anybody wanna move to Greece?"

I spoke earlier of the early experiment in this country with socialism in the commonwealth of Massachusetts. The governor at that time, William Bradford, decreed that the early settlers, the Pilgrims, all will receive equal plots of land, and the fruits of everyone's labors will be shared by all.

Here I will try to do my best John Wayne imitation phonetically,

"How did that work out for ya, Pilgrim?"

FOOTBALL: THE EARLY LEADERS

JIM THORPE/POP WARNER

Jim Thorpe was called one of, if not the greatest athlete of the early 20th century. He excelled at football, track, baseball and even basketball, but it was football that first brought him to national attention, playing for an American Indian school, Carlisle.

He was born in what is now northern Oklahoma as a member of the Sauk-Fox Indian tribes.

His father, Hiram was a big man for the times, standing over six feet tall and weighing over 225 pounds. His wife Charlotte, bore him 9 children, Jim was born with a twin bother Charles.

Can you imagine the literal pain of delivering nine children back in that time? There were few hospitals, no epidurals; child birth was a dangerous proposition. That Jim's mother survived bearing 9 children bears a testament to his work ethic.

Jim and his twin brother, were born on May 22, 1887. They were inseparable until Charles untimely death, caused by a typhoid epidemic.

Some think this shock at the age of ten, of losing his twin, is what made Thorpe become a bit withdrawn in personality.

Many of the greatest of us sometime have to start from meager beginnings, to then appreciate our later stations in life.

Entering the Carlisle school for Indians at the age of 16, Jim would spend the better part of 7 years there. Thought to be too little when he first approached the football coach at Carlisle, he was told to come back later. He decided to pursue football anyway, playing for a local trade shop team, the tailors. I guess you might say that "suited" him at the time...............or not.

On December 6, 1906, the legendary Pop Warner, a University of Georgia grad,(GO DAWGS!) his name now synonymous with youth football, returned to Carlisle as head coach, where he first met Jim Thorpe. Thorpe ran like no other.

Speaking of Thorpe, it was said by a famous sportswriter of the times,

"He moved with such ease, even at a saunter," that legendary sportswriter Grantland Rice remarked that Thorpe moved "like a breeze"

On one fall afternoon Pop Warner watched his future star walk across the filed on his way to a trade shop football game. Thorpe was dressed in overalls and gyms shoes when he happened upon some high jumpers, from the track team, practicing the high jump.

The bar was set at 5 feet nine inches and nobody at the school had ever cleared that height.

"Can I try?" Thorpe asked.

The varsity boys laughed at him, and said to go ahead and give it a try They stood by and waited for him to crash into the bar.

After a couple of practice strides toward the bar, he took off and scissor-ed his body over the bar. (The Scissor Step was the dominant technique of the times. This was decades before the introduction of the now standard "Fosbury Flop")

As Thorpe easily cleared the 5'9" height, the varsity boy's jaws dropped, and stared at him as he walked away.

If you have confidence in your abilities, there is no telling to what heights you can take yourself, your school, your company or even your nation.

Let's keep the bar high.

Under the coaching of Pop Warner, the Carlisle football team thrived, due in part to Warner's penchant for innovation. Prior to his inventions, the offense for a football team was pretty much a steamroller mentality, where the bigger team would succeed by literally pushing the opposition down the field. So a bigger team had a real advantage. But Pop Warner, recognizing the quickness of his smaller Carlisle squad, came up with innovations that we take for granted today. It was Jim Thorpe's ability to run, pass or kick that allowed Warner to offer these many innovations, and successfully outwit the often larger opposition.

Warner moved his fullback out wide to outflank the opposing tackle, forming what would be called "the single wing" It opened up a world of possibilities.

There was also a little used innovation called, The Forward Pass" (nah, it'll never catch on....)

Up until 1906, if a player threw the football it was pitched underhanded or lobbed through the air end over end. Though the forward pass was legalized that season, most teams felt it too unfamiliar to use it more than occasionally.

The first downfield overhand spiral was completed on September 5, 1906 by Brett Favre.

(Just kidding, Favre was decades from beginning his career in 1906, he didn't come around until 1921 or was it 1991?)

The first pass was actually thrown by St Louis College quarterback Bradley Robinson to teammate Jack Schneider, in a game against Carroll College.

This conflicts with the popular thought that the first forward pass was credited to Notre Dame in 1913, and the duo of Knute Rockne and Gus Dorais

By the fall of 1907, Pop Warner put his imagination to work to weave the pass into his offensive system. The beauty of his system lay in the fact that as his teamed lined up, no one could know whether the team was going to run, pass or kick.

Warner even taught his quarterback to sprint out to the left or right on pass plays, thus buying more time to throw. Hence the "roll out" was born.

Warner was an innovator, both on and off the field.

When Carlisle refused to assist in the expense of uniforms for his football team, he found a way to take care of that problem. He noticed that the school purchased it's canned goods from a local food canning operation. Warner, not one to back down from a problem, promptly purchased a portion of that local business and used the profits of his business interest to supply his team.

He didn't saddle anyone else with is problem. He didn't complain that other schools had nice new uniforms, on the contrary, he looked for a solution and went out and got it done.

It is a great lesson for all, for all time. If you want to solve a problem, find a way and work at it. Don't expect a hand out.

COWBOYS VERSUS INDIANS

In the fall of 1914, Carlisle, had become a rising power in college football and one to be reckoned with, would face the undefeated West Point- US military academy (Army) team. The Cadets were led in part by future president Dwight D. Eisenhower. Though relegated to the junior varsity, (this is not the ISIS terror group that President Obama called the JV) as an underclassman, the scrappy halfback worked hard to improve on his 155lb frame. By the fall of 1914, he would be a major force for the Cadets football team. That size, 155lbs sounds small, but considering this was over 100 years ago, heck he could have been a kinebacker.

Eisenhower was a member of the class of 1915.
This class of 164 men, would produce 58 generals, including World War II leader, Omar Bradley.
Clearly the Army team was not shy on leadership.
What would this group think of the leadership of today's commander in chief?

There was much on the line with this game. Both teams having enjoyed very successful seasons, were vying for the title of the best team in the nation.

Carlisle was outmanned by the larger Army squad. While sizes of players were less in those days, the Carlisle team was grossly undersized. In fact in the many years that Pop Warner coached them, the Indians would only once average more than 170lbs per player.

Clearly it would take a supreme effort to win this game, and perhaps some innovations, would make it happen.

Football would be changed forever by Carlisle, and the performance it would give.

Having received the first kickoff, Carlisle came to the line of scrimmage.

What happened next is football history.

Coach Pop Warner knew that he needed something special to take on Army. He chose this game to debut a new formation, what is now called the "double wing". Can you imagine the look on the faces of the Cadets, when they lined up in this strange, never before seen, formation.

In this line up, he had both of his halfbacks line up toward the line of scrimmage, outside of the defensive tackles. This was a huge departure from the norm. This gave Carlisle a near infinite number of options. Led by Jim Thorpe, QB Gus Welch and others, on any offensive snap they could run, reverse, fake, pass, pitch, and any number of combinations. It began a new era in football. The old guard, steamrolling offenses of the past, would be no match for this new way of playing the game.

Dwight Eisenhower played both ways for the cadets, but this was common in those days. He started at halfback and at linebacker, where along with teammate Charles Benedict, worked to harass and stop running back Jim Thorpe.

On one play as Thorpe ran the ball, Eisenhower and Benedict both hit him at the same time, the old 'high and low',(now highly illegal) and this left the running back for Carlisle shaken and unable to get up. But he got back up. (Good lesson, huh?)

Once when Ike and Benedict seemed to have Thorpe cornered, he stopped short, resulting in the two Army linebackers to hit head on, ala the Three Stooges, allowing Thorpe to run on past. Both linebackers were removed from the game and as it turns out, it was one of the last games that Eisenhower would play.

The following week, in a game against Tufts, he would sprain his knee. When he would re-injure the knee jumping his horse in the riding ring, he was forced to give up football. While West Point lost a football player, they gained a military leader.

As the game wore on, the Cadets were beaten as they had not been beaten before.

Jim Thorpe had a spectacular catch of a 40 yard pass, where he jumped two feet into the air, twisting his body to catch the ball between two cadet defenders.

The final score was 27-6, but it could have been much worse. Carlisle did not allow Army a first down in the second half and had the ball four more times on the Army 5 yard line without scoring.

This time the Indians had beaten the Cowboys.

GEORGE GIPP

George Gipp, was tall for the times, when he first made his debut on the football field for Notre Dame in 1916. A Michigan native from the U-P, (upper peninsula), he was six feet tall and 175 lbs. He was the type of rambler, gambler (he did play a lot of pool) that made the game such a wide open sport back then. With George anything could happen and usually did.

One great example was in one of his first football games for the Fighting Irish.

There was about two minutes remaining in a freshman game against Western State Normal (now Western Michigan). For those of you born after the 1960's, the protocol in college athletics until the late sixties and early 1970's, was that freshman were not allowed to participate on varsity teams. Officially,

"In 1968, the NCAA allowed freshman eligibility in all sports, except football and basketball and extended the rule to those sports effective with the 1972-1973 academic year."

I guess they wanted the "student athletes"
to adjust to college and get their grades in order.
Has the term 'student-athlete" become an oxy-moron?

Now, back to the action.

The Notre Dame – Western State Normal score was tied 7-7 in this particular freshman game with about two minutes to go.

Notre Dame faced a 4th and 15 on their own 38 yard line. The situation called for a punt.

"Punt it George" barked QB Frank Thomas, relaying the call from the Notre Dame coach.

"Why settle for a tie" Gipp asked, let me try for a drop kick, I'm sure I can make it"

Gipp's teammates smiled but the quarterback was not amused. A "Drop Kick", much in fashion back then happened when the punter dropped the ball to the ground and as it bounced up, the punter then kicked it toward the goal, as a field goal. You didn't line up for a field goal back then as you do today.

"Just punt the ball, that's it", said the quarterback, angrily, one last time.

Notre Dame went into punt formation and the ball was snapped. Taking a high snap from center, Gipp, dropped the ball to the ground and then with a powerful thrust from his right leg, kicked the ball bouncing up from the ground and sent a dropkick straight down the middle of the field. It was a low end over end kick that sailed down the filed until it cleared the crossbar 62 yards from the line of scrimmage to make it the second longest field goal ever. (The record at that time was 65 yards)

Technically though, since Gipp kicked it from his 31 yard line, it was actually a 69 yard kick.

On the field Gipp was mobbed by his teammates for his improbable field goal, which would turn out to be decisive, in their 10-7 victory.

Knute Rockne was a chemistry professor and an assistant football coach. One would assume he enjoyed a degree of satisfaction, knowing that he had strongly suggested that the reluctant Gipp try out for football. Rockne had barely gotten to know Gipp. The Notre Dame coach, very young at 28, was just 7 years older than his budding player. Rockne felt that this was most likely not going to be the first act of disobedience on a football filed, or anywhere else by the unlikely hero from a small town in Michigan's UP, Laurium, Michigan.

Was Gipp's kick a long shot? What were the odds of making it? Should he have gone for it?

Hey, you don't know until you try. Push fear aside and go for it........it could happen.

RED GRANGE #77

The famous Red Grange, old #77, the "Gallopin Ghost" as he was called, for his ability to change direction and seemingly vanish, was one of America's stars of the Golden Age of Sports, back in the 1920s. But the golden age did not mean that these early gridiron greats had it easier, on the contrary, they often had to improvise, so that the game could survive.

After a stellar gridiron career at the University of Illinois, Grange went on to professional football with the Chicago Bears, the much heralded, "Monsters of the Midway"

Red Grange was so popular in college, that immediately after signing him as a professional, the Chicago Bears put together an extremely tough 19 game, 67 day barnstorming tour, to make money. That is an average of two games a week, un heard of these days plus, back then, protective equipment was present in name only.

It was Dec 18th, 1932, and the NFL championship game between the Chicago Bears and the Portsmouth (Ohio) Spartans looked like it was not going to happen, thanks to Mother Nature.
The game was scheduled outside at Wrigley Field in Chicago, but heavy snow made the field unplayable, forcing the game to be moved indoors to the Chicago Stadium.

The setting was intimate with just 11,198 fans. People sitting in the front row could hear what was being said on the field, without the aid of microphones.

The floor was concrete, softened a bit thanks to a layer of dirt and elephant dung taken from the nearby Salvation Army circus.

(I guess you could say the conditions "stunk")

The field was too short, so each time a team crossed midfield it was penalized 20 yards, making the field 100 yards long. No field goals were allowed.

The teams did not want to run into the walls. These were only about 2 feet from the side of the stadium. Both teams agreed to bring the ball in from the walls about 15 yards.

As a result "Hash Marks" were born.

Chicago looked like a shoo in to win the game. They had the better defense and the Spartans best player and league leading scorer, left his job to take an off season job as a basketball coach. The pay, even in championship games was miniscule by today's standards. Each member of the winning team was paid the princely sum of $210.

Red Grange was nearly knocked out in the first quarter but later returned to the game. The players wore soft leather helmets called "No Knock Off's. The leather, not much more than the thickness of a heavy leather coat, provided little protection considering the bruising tackles of the era.

The Bears, had the ball on the Spartans 2 yard line, but they couldn't seem to score, until Bronko Nagurski, faked a run, then backpedaled, throwing a pass to Red. Red, dead tired and woozy had fallen in the end zone, but always on his game in the clutch, caught the pass for the win.

Football was a tough way to make a living back then, but the options in the depth of the Depression were few and far between, so you played with pain and injuries. Many players would turn out to be debilitated, later in life, due to these injuries.

There were no players unions back then and the owners could pay you or cut you. Red Grange, as did many players of the era, suffered countless injuries but played relatively long careers.

Because of all of the nasty blows he had incurred as a player, Red later in life contracted Parkinsons. This is the disease suffered by many athletes that were subjected to many blows to the head.

BE READY TO IMPROVISE

It was December 28th 1958, The New York Giants met the Baltimore Colts under the lights at Yankee Stadium for the NFL Championship.

It was special as it was the first championship game to go into overtime and also the first time that it was aired on this young medium called "Television."

Late in the 4th quarter, the Colts were trailing 17-14, when Baltimore kicker Steve Myhra came to the line of scrimmage. He was facing just 19, but seemingly 19 long yards for a field goal to tie the game. George Shaw was the holder for Myhra, who was thinking what a cold winter it would be back in North Dakota if he missed this kick. He thought also of the Giants attempt to block a kick in the first quarter, and vowed to get this one off quicker.

Shaw took a knee and scratched an "X" in the turf where he planned to set the ball. Very scientific don't you think? X marks the spot.

For Myhra it would be a 19 yard try. There wasn't much time to fret over it, so he readied himself for the kick.

The ball was snapped, Shaw placed it and Myhra took one step and placed the wide edge of his cleats in to the ball.

This was a time when all kickers were still straight drop leg kickers, as the first soccer style kicker Pete Gogolak, had yet appeared on the NFL scene.

Myhra looked up just in time to see the ball sail cleanly over the crossbar.

In Baltimore, it was learned, that a driver listening on the radio ran his car into a telephone pole.

The game was tied 17-17 as players from both sides ran toward the locker rooms to escape being mobbed by the raucous crowd.

But wait, the game wasn't over.

The NFL was about to play its first ever "sudden-death" overtime game. Hard to believe that there was no sudeen death OT, huh?

The largest audience to ever witness a pro football game was watching and listening. The recently deceased NFL Commissioner Bert Bell was in heaven, grinning like the Cheshire Cat.

The overtime progressed and found Baltimore driving, and with a catch by wide receiver Raymond Berry, they landed at the Giants 8 yard line. It looked tough now for the Giants, whose backs were against the wall.

And then it happened................

Just as the game appeared to be nearing it's climax, America's TV sets went gray, losing their picture

NBC had literally lost its' (cable) connection. Someone in the crowd, milling around behind the end zone had kicked loose the network cable and disconnected America. Unthinkable now, in the days of satellite TV signals.

The Colts broke the huddle and approached the line of scrimmage. In years to come games would regularly stop for commercials or broadcast emergencies, but with the medium of Television, in its infancy, the game would proceed with or without television coverage. Hopefully the TV men were prepared.

From the radio announcer then came this amusing announcement: "Play will be held up now as a fan is running on the field with three of New York's finest in hot pursuit, trying to corner the guy."

The runner a giddy looking young man gave the cops a good run. He moved well, covering most of the field, before additional policemen from the opposite end zone intercepted him.

More from the announcer, "and now they get him (chuckling) down at about the 22 yard line. Now there are 4 or 5 policemen escorting him off the field."

"God-dang, shouldn't be getting me", said the soon to be arrested man, "You should be getting that number nineteen Unitas, he's the one that's killin' us!" Obviously the intruder was a Giants fan.

Newspaper reports would later report about the "drunk" that held up the action, just as the game hung in the balance. This delay was just enough time for the network engineers to reconnect the cable. TV sets across the country came back to life in time to see the Colts line up at the eight yard line, with a first and goal to go.

Nothing was missed. Quite a lucky break for the network, or was it?

For you see, the man was not drunk.

In fact, he hadn't been drinking, he had been working. His name was Stan Rotkiewicz, He was a business manager for NBC news and on game day worked for the network as a statistician. Stan had played some college football and in the service of his network, had quite nicely, dusted off some of his old college football moves, running long enough to allow the network engineers to plug back in America. The TV executives were clever.

Two months earlier, in an article about TV coverage of football, in the New York Times,

A CBS producer had speculated about ways his network could stop play on the field, in a pinch.

"Maybe we could cue a drunk to go out and interrupt things" Ahhh.

Things are not always as they seem, skim milk masquerades as cream.

Not sure that that line has any football relevance, but it came to mind.

In football, and in life, it pays to be ready, and have the confidence to improvise. This doesn't mean that you change things up entirely, that you discard the basics that brought you here, but rather to use those basics, add a wrinkle, and go for it, with the confidence that you know you have done the work, and that you have faith in your system. This faith leads to success.

HAVE A SENSE OF HUMOR

In daily life, if we can't laugh now and then at ourselves or make light of a situation we might just go crazy.

Even in the height of battle on the playing field, there is room for a lighter moment. Take your job seriously but don't take yourself too seriously is a great maxim by which to live life.

In the early part of the 20th century the Carlisle Indians, led by Jim Thorpe, dominated the college football scene. They took on and beat many of the eastern football powerhouses of the day, including Penn, Harvard, Pitt, and Syracuse. On one fall day this included a drubbing of then mighty Lehigh University.

The game was so far gone that Carlisle even began announcing its plays to the opposition.

When they did score, one of the Carlisle linemen would issue this apology.

It was William Garlow, one of the most intellectual members of the squad, who, after a score, would stand up and announce:

"Gentleman, this hurts me as much you, but it appears the ball is over the goal line. Nobody regrets it more than we do. If there was a way of correcting this error on our part, we would be glad to do it. But there is not the slightest doubt about the situation that confronts us here. It's a touchdown."

"We would very much prefer that this were happening to someone else, but the facts are clear and you will see that the little pellet is resting very securely behind the white line. We regret it, I am sure you regret it, and I hope that nothing happening here will spoil what for us has been a very pleasant afternoon"

Players on both sides were overcome by spasms of laughter.

Be serious about your job, but having a sense of humor, will help carry you through both the scores and the fumbles of daily life.

EARLY, TESTED LEADERS IN AMERICA

GEORGE WASHINGTON

"First in War, First in Peace, First in the hearts of his Countrymen"
George Washington.

Imagine stepping into a job that had no precedents, no guidelines, no history.

This job would prove to become the most important job in the world.

(No, I am not talking about the head football coaching position at the University of Alabama, although some residents of that state may take issue with me on that.)

I am talking about the Presidency of the United States, and George Washington.

Washington was the first, hence there was no history. Just as Pop Warner would later learn as head coach of the University of Carlisle football team, this was both a blessing and a curse.

As the first anything, one can propose any set of guidelines, strategies, rules etc. But likewise, there is no history from which to learn. There are no playbooks, no game films, no scouting reports.

Successful leaders are called back to one simple point. That point is principles and following those to make decisions, despite what anyone says.

In 1789 George Washington was elected unanimously as the first President of the United States. Washington helped shape the office's future role and powers, as well as set both formal and informal precedents, for future presidents.

Washington believed that it was necessary to strike a delicate balance between making the presidency powerful enough to function effectively in a national government, while also avoiding any image of establishing a monarchy or dictatorship.

In the process he significantly influenced the path of the presidency moving forward, setting standards in all aspects, including political power, military practice and economic policy.

Can you imagine if you were chosen to be the first head coach of an institution. The decisions you make would affect the program for years to come. Washington was that head coach, the first head coach of the United States of America.

"Washington-First in war, first in peace and last in the American League"

(Lament over the woeful Washington Senators major league baseball team that seem to continually languish in last place back in the 1950's and 1960's)

No real connection to this book, but it's one of those comments I have always remembered.

I will take a literary "mulligan" here.

ABRAHAM LINCOLN
(THE CIVIL WAR)

Long recognized as one of America's greatest President, Abe Lincoln was responsible for holding the US together during one of the toughest times this nation has ever faced, the Civil War.

Following the attack at Fort Sumter in April of 1861, Lincoln faced a challenge no other President had faced. The South, wanting to be free of the overreach of the Federal Government, (The North), collected a band of states and agreed to secede.

The Civil War had begun.

Lincoln faced many challenges, not unlike the multi pronged attack that is faced by a football coach in a struggling program. When a football team is losing, there is always an instant call for him to be fired, this coming from the press, the alumni and even the students. Despite these constant challenges, a football coach needs to remain true to his principles, to keep the team moving ahead, in an effort to regain positive results. He has to drop back to his core principles. This is what Lincoln did.

Having read my 7th grade history and later a course in college, I assumed that when the Civil War started, that the nation united as one behind Lincoln, in his fight to save the union. Upon further investigation, I found out I was wrong.

The South sought help from Britain and France. Because of this, many northern business leaders and private groups urged the president to sit down with the Southern leaders and come up with a peace proposal. These northerners felt that it was better that the nation become two entities, rather than risk their business enterprises or family connections. I'm sure that modern presidents feel the same pressures to act on behalf of certain groups. Lincoln knew better.

Abe Lincoln had taken an oath to preserve, protect and maintain the sovereignty of the United States.

He resolved to do that, despite the many public and personal problems he faced. It has been suggested that the president suffered form bouts of depression. His life had been anything but easy.

In an 1859 autobiographical letter, Lincoln mentioned a near-death experience at age 10. He was kicked by a horse and nearly killed.

William Herndon, Lincoln's law partner, described the incident in his 1889 biography "Herndon's Lincoln: The True Story of a Great Life."

Young Abe was whipping the horse and yelling, "Get up, you old hussy" when "the old horse, resenting the continued harassment, elevated her shoeless hoof and struck the young engineer in the forehead, sending him to the dirt.

Lincoln was knocked unconscious and remained in that state until the next morning. With the "blood beginning to flow normally, his tongue struggled to loosen itself, his body jerked for an instant, and he awoke, blurting out the words 'you old hussy,' The last half of the sentence, had been interrupted by the mare's heel.

Edward J. Kempf, a neurologist, theorized in his 1965 book that the incident caused cerebral damage and contributed to the "melancholy" he felt throughout his life.

Lincoln was often described as suffering from melancholy (depression) during his life. In looking at his own letters one can conclude that he was probably prone to bouts of depression. William

Herndon said of him, "He was a sad-looking man; his melancholy dripped from him as he walked. His apparent gloom impressed his friends, and created sympathy for him. He was gloomy, abstracted, joyous and often rather humorous by turns; but I do not think he knew what real joy was for many years. The perpetual look of sadness was his most prominent feature."

Lincoln likely would have been diagnosed with clinical depression if he were alive today, wrote Joshua Wolf Shenk in his 2005 book "Lincoln's Melancholy,"

However, Shenk also stated that Lincoln's depression drove him to become a great president. During those tough days of the Civil War, Shenk says, "The suffering he had endured lent him clarity and conviction, creative skills in the face of adversity, and a faithful humility that helped him guide the nation through its greatest peril."

Lincoln suffered many losses during his lifetime. He was engaged to be married as a young man only to have his first love in life die very young.

Anne Rutledge was a beautiful, intelligent, free spirit. Lincoln met her in the town of New Salem, IL in the early 1830's

Anne Rutledge died suddenly in August 1835 of typhoid. Another resident, John Hill, said that "Lincoln bore up under it very well until some days afterwards as a heavy rain fell. Another friend, Henry McHenry testified that after her death, "he seemed quite changed, he seemed retired, & loved solitude, he seemed wrapped in profound thought, somewhat unaware of events around him.

Mr. Lincoln was grievously affected by her death. "The deepest gloom and melancholy settled over his mind.

He would often say to his friends: "My heart is buried in the grave with that dear girl." He would often go and sit by her grave and read a little pocket Testament he carried with him

William Wallace "Willie" Lincoln (December 21, 1850 – February 20, 1862) was the third son of Abraham Lincoln and Mary Todd Lincoln. He died of an illness at the tender age of 11.

Willie and brother Tad became ill in early 1862. Tad recovered, but Willie's condition fluctuated from day to day. The most likely cause of the illness was typhoid fever. This was often contracted by consumption of fecal contaminated food/water. The White House drew its water from the Potomac River, along which thousands of soldiers and horses were camped. Gradually Willie weakened, and his parents spent much time at his bedside. Finally, on Wednesday, February 20, 1862, at 5:00 p.m., Willie died. Abraham said, "My poor boy. He was too good for this earth. God has called him home."

I know that he is much better off in heaven, but then we loved him so much.

Both parents were deeply affected. His father did not return to work for three weeks. Willie's younger brother, Tad, cried for nearly a month because he and Willie were very close. Lincoln sent out no official correspondence for four days. Mary was so distraught that Lincoln feared for her sanity.

Now many of you Lincoln fans recall this information about our 16th president. It goes to prove a point about staying the course.

All of this and Lincoln was still faced with the daily struggle of holding a fragile nation together.

Suddenly the job of being a head football coach sounds pretty easy, in comparison.

"Get me the University President on the phone......

FOOTBALL NEARLY ABOLISHED, INJURED, BUT CAME BACK STRONGER

If not for an injury to the President Teddy Roosevelt's son, football may have ceased to exist.

In 1904 there were 21 fatalities and more than 200 serious injuries in the game.

In today's game we worry, and rightfully so about concussions, back then you worried about being killed.

It was a dirty business. Hey, just one more way in which politics and football are the same!

In a game in 1905, Theodore Roosevelt, Jr, playing for Harvard's freshman team was laid out in a game against Yale, and even had his nose broken.

This left his father fed up with the brutal mass play in a game he had defended to this point.

In the 1905 season there were another 18 deaths and 149 serious injuries reported and an outcry to ban the game swept the nation.

It goes to show all, how the football community has changed over the years. Now players of all ages are noted and examined thoroughly even if it is suspected that a concussion may have been suffered. Improvements had to be made to save the game. Just as adjustments need to be made by citizens of the U.S. and their elected representatives, from time to time, to make this country a better place.

President Roosevelt summoned representatives from the college game to the White House to establish ground rules that would lessen the brutality of the game. He was fed up with the brutal play that threatened to ruin a game he enjoyed and believed in. He often defended the game.

Of all the games, I personally like football the best, and would rather see my boys play it than any other. I have no patience with people who declaim against it."

In late December, representatives of 28 major colleges met to form the National Intercollegiate Football Conference, charging a 7 member rules committee with developing a cleaner, safer sport. (From, "The real Americans"-Sally Jenkins)

Some of the rules adopted will seem familiar to fans of today,

- Mass plays were forbidden (steamrolling down the field as one mass)
- Teams had to move ten yards for a first down instead of five, which took the emphasis off of pure strength in the center of the field.

But most inventive of all, the forward pass was legalized, though with an inhibitor, a team that tried to throw and failed would be penalized 15 yards.

Contrast that action with the way this current Obama administration often deals with those that try and fail today in their work lives, where those that can't make it, or can't complete a pass, per se, are not penalized as were these early football pioneers, but are given government handouts rather than encouraged to work harder.

The recent administration does not want people to succeed on their own merits. They want them beholden to the government. And for those that do succeed, rather than hold them up as an example, these people are many times ridiculed as not being worthy of their efforts, insert here the infamous Obama line "You didn't build that", here. Rather than unite and encourage, the current leaders wants to divide and discourage achievement in this country.

Where would the forward pass be if after a failed attempt, it wasn't tried again? Where would the game be if that portion of the offense was not experimented with and encouraged? Where would this country be if hard work and persistence wasn't encouraged?

I wonder if many in the current Administration have ever tried to throw a pass.

AMERICA, ABOLISHMENT NEAR?

Now some will say that America has just reached a stage that we are now a different country and we need to realize that we are not the great land of opportunity that we once were. We need to settle for what we have become.

Balderdash!

What has happened is that a combination of complacency and apathy has overtaken the US. Increased frustration with our politicians, poor if any leadership at the executive level, has led us to several consecutive quarters of minimal economic growth, People have had to settle for part time jobs if they can get them, many have left the workforce and have cozied up to ever enlarged government programs.

We are down in the game and we have decided that our opponent is just too tough and so we have resigned ourselves to second place, which by the way in a football game, is called, the loser.

Apathy in this country has hit an all time high. The bitter partisan in fighting of Congress has left many Americans dispirited and discouraged, What's the use?

We expend all of our energy fighting against each other and nothing gets done in the way of solving today's problems and getting this country back on track.

Back in 1989 Lou Holtz, then Notre Dames head coach was playing a critical game against USC and ran into the same problem of channeling his team's efforts in the right direction,

Before the game even began the coach knew his team was in trouble, as his team succumbed to the taunts of the opposition, forgetting his instructions to keep their head in the game, and a fight erupted. Holtz was outraged.

In the pre game locker room he chastised his team for letting their guard down, for letting the outcry from the other team make them lose their focus. This is something we can all relate to in real life.

So what did the coach do.......

He rallied his team, got their energy and their anger back up, but this time he was behind them, urging them to channel that anger toward the opposition.

He was not upset so much over the pre-game fisticuffs, but rather over their inept play. They were distracted and took their eye off of the target.

He vented his feelings over the poor performance and the history of this storied program,

They deserved better,

When the team took the filed in the third quarter, their attitude had done a complete 180. It was a completely different team, that went on to the field, to start the second half, and win the game that day 28-24.

Now we may have been lucky enough to have been a part of that Notre Dame team that day, or perhaps being a ND fan, we can recall that great comeback.

But what we can all take away from this is what an attitude adjustment could do for this nation.

We are mired in an environment of crushing regulations for small business owners, of a constant attempt by the White House to divide this nation into the "Haves" and "Have Nots." Remember the big uproar and ensuing demonstrations in 2013 over the hated "One Per Cent?" How dare someone succeed at business. Rather than encourage the nation's team, its citizens, to fight back to take that hand up and begin working to get back to where we want to be, the current government finds it easiest to work to divide the country. In this manner, the White House and some members of Congress do not have to offer any "new plays" or innovations.

Rather they deflect their poor performance by pointing at the other team, those that are successful.

When have you ever heard more use of the term "That's not fair?"

Who said Life is Fair?

Can you imagine if coach Lou Holtz had taken this approach? What if he had decided that rather than try to rally his team in the game against USC, that he had instead began complaining to the refs that USC is not playing fair, that they should penalize USC for playing too hard and succeeding. How do you think his players would have reacted?

How would the ND fans have reacted? It's a chain reaction of sorts.

Many may have decided that USC was not playing fair and that they, the ND team were "victims" What a disheartening scene that second half would have been.

Nothing is easier in life than deciding that we are victims of some injustice or disservice.

This attitude takes the onus away from us and our performance and puts the 'blame' on others. So we as a nation take the easy approach to life, we complain, and point fingers at others, like the One Percenters, it's their fault.

This nation so needs a good pep talk and a new head coach.

Hey coach, quit telling us that 7% unemployment is the new norm, (rates for youths and minorities are in the double digits) Quit telling us that what we had in the past we didn't deserve.

Quit pointing fingers at the winning team and saying
"Hey those guys aren't playing Fair"

What if Nick Saban at Alabama, had given his players this talk at halftime of a tough game,

Hey, you guys got lucky with those scores in the first half, you didn't deserve those, you may as well get used to the fact that you are no longer a good football team, and expect to be a second rate squad.

Nothing could be further from the truth when it comes to Coach Saban.

Even after the National Championship win in 2012, he let his players know the very next day that, while they should be congratulated for their efforts in beating Notre Dame, they need to remember that it's time to get back to work.

Is it any wonder that US businesses are looking to set up shop outside the country?

Is it any wonder that businesses are sitting on record piles of cash, afraid to invest it in new production facilities. Is it any wonder that new employment remains stagnant?

It is because this country does not know what direction the government has in mind.

Maybe the "prez" will continue his efforts to cripple the US Coal industry. Maybe he will limit the number of drilling permits for offshore oil rigs. Perhaps he will continue to push for his "Cap in Trade" program which will cripple American business and cause the energy costs for Americans to soar. How about the Iran nuclear deal?

Are you getting the picture.

How am I supposed to enter the playing field each day, when I have no idea how the coach is next going to try and hamstring my efforts?

We need a new coach, we need new leadership. We need someone that will remind us to get back to the basics of hard work and personal responsibility.'

I wonder how that Notre Dame game would have ended had Lou Holtz not taken the course he chose? Hmmmm.........

STAYING THE COURSE –LOMBARDI

No coach did as much to emphasize the need for basic, fundamentals like Vince Lombardi, the highly successful coach of the Green Bay Packers.

Noted as one of the "7 blocks of Granite" for his offensive line play in the 1930's, for Fordham University, Lombardi emphasized team play and an absolute adherence to learning to do things right, not just the first time, but every time.

In 1959 Lombardi was named head coach and general manager of a woeful Green Bay packer organization. Following the end of the 1958 season, the Packers had gone through 4 head coaches, and compiled a record of 10-39-1

Their record for 1958 was 1-10-1.

This prompted the legendary sportswriter Red Smith to write "The Packers underwhelmed ten opponents, overwhelmed one and whelmed one" (From, "The year that changed the game" -Jonathan Rand)

Vince Lombardi brought his own philosophy to Green Bay. His practices we're not long, usually just 90 minutes, short by today's standards, but were quite intense.

Unlike many of his peers, Lombardi's playbook was relatively simple. His thought was not to out think the opponent with endless schemes and razzle-dazzle, but rather to run a simple set of plays. But he made sure, his teams would learn to execute those plays to perfection each time they were run.

When teaching blocking and tackling, the coach was a perfectionist.

Here is an excerpt from Lombardi's first speech to his team the night before their first practice together.

"With every fiber of my body, I've go to make you the best football player I can make you. And I'll try.

And I'll try. And if I don't succeed I'll try again, And I'll try again. And you have got to give everything that is in you. You've go to keep yourself in prime condition, because fatigue makes cowards of us all. We are going to win some games. Do you know why? Because, you are going to have confidence in my system."

By being alert you are going to make fewer mistakes than your opponents. By working harder you are going to out execute, out block and out-tackle every team that comes your way.

I've never been a losing coach and I don't intend to start here. There is nobody big enough to think he has the team made or can do what he wants. Trains and plans are going in and out of Green Bay every day, and he'll be on one of them.

I won't. I'm going to find 36 men, who have the pride to make any sacrifice to win. There are such men. If they are not here, I'll get them. If you are not one, if you don't want to play, then you might as well leave now."

Later, Lombardi admitted that he hoped that none of his players would walk out, and none did.

Though few immediately warmed up to him, most could appreciate what he was trying to accomplish.

To me, nothing better explains a system that breeds success in this great country than this speech by Lombardi.

When everyone does his/her job, when people pull together for a common cause, then that is when success is attained. Lombardi would not have achieved the success of those great Packer teams if half of his players decided that they should contribute.

So why, as a country should we expect to get this country back on track, when some our leaders continue to speak not in terms of teamwork but rather, of a system that is "Not Fair", because those that work hard are successful, but those that have not, are not.

People respond to someone that has a plan, or a system, that can guarantee success. Sometimes we need that little kick, or bit of motivation to get ourselves in gear.

Paul Hornung was an All American running back at Notre Dame back in the 1950's before being drafted by Green Bay. He played for two dismal Green Bay teams before Lombardi was named head coach.

Hornung later recalled what a positive influence Coach Lombardi was on him.

"Vince changed my life, and he came along at just the right time. My first two years with the Packers were so unhappy and unsatisfying, that I was ready to quit and do something else. I needed a sense of purpose direction in my life to keep from drifting and that's exactly what Lombardi gave me.

He told me right away I was going to be his starting left halfback. No more would I have to be switching positions. And he told me that if he didn't make it playing left halfback for him, I would not make it in pro football."

It was as simple as that. That challenge motivated me and gave me the focus I needed. From then on, I was committed to being the best professional football player I could be.

THE PACKER SWEEP

Sometimes the most successful strategy is the most obvious. We too often expect a new, totally unexpected economic strategy from our leaders, to jump start or re-ignite a crumbling or stagnant economy. But, that's not really necessary, is it?

Vince Lombardi's favorite play was the power sweep. As the ball was hiked, the guards, most notably, Jerry Kramer and Fuzzy Thurston would pull to one side leading the way for the ball carrier, usually Paul Hornung,

A few interesting facts about the Packer Power Sweep were:

The Packers knew it was coming.
The opponent knew it was coming.
The Packers knew that the opponent knew it was coming.
The opponent knew, that the Packers knew, that they knew, it was coming.
And still, it was unstoppable.

As Coach Vince Lombardi stated,
"Every team arrives at a lead play, one they can count on, their bread and butter play. Ours is the power sweep. It is the play the team must make go and the one the opponents must stop. My number one play has been the power sweep. There is nothing fancy about it, it's just a yard gainer.

But on the sideline, watching the play develop, you can hear those linebackers and defensive backs yelling, Sweep, Sweep, and almost see their eyes pop out as those guards turn up field after them.

The ball carrier on the sweep is the left halfback and I have been fortunate to coach a couple of good ones who made the sweep their personal play, Paul Hornung and Frank Gifford. Though neither had blinding speed, they were both quick intelligent runners who could control their running, so that used their blockers and got every possible yard out of each play."

The Bottom line is this, if you have a common sense strategy, involving hard work, but measurable results, why not go with it. When everyone does their job, good things happen.

This is an easily understood, yet successful strategy for reviving the US economy.

Let your blockers clear the field (of the endless regulation and taxes) and let the runner (the economy) explode downfield.

Everyone knows it works, and everyone knows it's coming......
....................Touchdown.

USA COMEBACKS AND
TURN AROUNDS

This country has seen many tough, dark times.

There have been depressions in the 1800's, Bank panics in the late 1800's and early 1900's and of course the great Depression of the 1920's and 30's, the Recessions in the early 1980's, the dot com bust and the real estate bubble burst most recently.

What caused these? Well, the causes of each are as varied as were the standard of living at the time.

But one theme that rings throughout each period is a variance from the core principles of the times.

One catalyst for the Great Depression in addition to some over regulation was speculation on the part of many investors at the time. After the War, the economy took off and many people were caught up in the euphoria of the times, including the stock market. One could purchase any number of shares of a stock "on margin", or by borrowing against the future gains of the stock, sometimes paying as little as 10% down, Since there was no end to how high the Market would go, who worried about a downside, everything was going up.

Many railroad stocks and auto company stocks mirrored the false promise of great gains as did the dot com stocks of the late 1990's.

That was where anything remotely related to the computer age was thought to have tremendous value. We all saw where that went.

Many of us witnessed first hand also the great real estate collapse of 2007. Again the over reaching hand of government entered in to stir up trouble.

It was thought by many political leaders, especially many Democrats, that everyone should own a house, and as such banks were pressured by the government to make loans to anyone wanting to get into a house, regardless of whether or not they were financially qualified.

One could qualify for a loan equal to 125% of the perceived value of the house, with little or no credit qualification.

As a result, after a while these loans had to be called, as people could not meet their obligations, and the financial house of cards came down.

What then ensued was not a return to the basics, but no, the government went for the razzle-dazzle play again with the infamous government bailout. This infusion of cash was going to shore up the defense and allow for more offense. But the billions and billions released into the economy did not result in a score, so to speak, and rather than admit that these trick plays were not working, the government continues to stand by the story that we need to continue to involve the citizens of this great nation in more assisted plays, rather than pull back and go with the basics.

Well at some point the fans and players reach a point and have had enough and they speak out.

Evidence of this is the mid term election of 2014.

There was a wave that swept the nation similar to the wave the sweeps around a football stadium. Just as the wave at a football game picks up momentum and then gains speed, so did the voters speaking their mind in this mid term election.

People have had enough of government talking about what's wrong with this country, how certain groups that pull their own weight are not doing enough. It's as if the offensive tackle that is grinding away at his position should be ashamed because he is not also handling the duties of the adjacent guard or center.

Citizens know what works, and what doesn't and the play calling of the administration since 2009, is not working.

The citizens of this country have spoken that they want a new leader, just as fans speak out when it's time to retire the head coach from the sidelines. Well, fortunately, this current coach Obama, as much as he would like to remain coach indefinitely, is on his way out.

The fans can now select a new one, one that knows the merits of hard work and will get back to basics, and not hamstring the citizens of this great country with needless regulations, just as a new head coach would not hamstring his players with needless, useless, exercises or drills.

FOOTBALL - AMERICA

Why do they both stay popular?

    Have you ever noticed that there are similar expressions in Football, and these are aphorisms we use to describe daily life?

    The trials and tribulations, we face on a daily basis here in America, bring us to use a lot of the same phrases, you'd hear in a football game.

    Some of these include:

- Our backs are against the Wall
- Its gut check time
- Trying for a Hail Mary
- Is it time to Punt?
- Time to Huddle Up
- The best Offense is a good Defense
- Protect your blind side
- Back to the Basics

(Feel free to add your own favorite here)

COACHES-PRESIDENTS

Running a football team or running a country, both jobs involve having the right people/players in place and the right staff, coaching or otherwise.

Many of our Presidents played football, and knew of the struggles involved in the game. These lessons were no doubt a part of the base of experience on which they drew, as they made decisions as President of the United States and Commander in Chief.

Five modern U.S. presidents played college football: Dwight Eisenhower (Army), Gerald Ford (Michigan), John Kennedy (Harvard), Richard Nixon (Whittier) and Ronald Reagan (Eureka).

DWIGHT EISENHOWER

As the supreme Allied commander in WW II, Eisenhower admitted that he looked for former football players to fill command spots.

He said, "I noted with satisfaction, how well ex-footballers seemed to fulfill leadership qualifications. These numbers included generals, Bradley, Keyes, Patton, Simpson, Van Fleet, Harmon, Hobbs, Jouett, Patch and Pritchard, and many others measured up. I cannot recall a single ex-footballer with whom I came in contact, who failed to meet every requirement.

Personally I think this was more than coincidental. I believe that football, almost more than any sport, tends to instill into men that victory come through hard---almost slavish work, team play, self confidence and an enthusiasm that amounts to dedication."

JOHN KENNEDY

John Kennedy played football at Harvard, but unlike his brothers who all excelled at the sport (both Robert & Edward were Harvard football lettermen), JFK did not progress beyond the JV team due to illness and injury in his freshmen year.

Despite his physical ailments, JFK remained as active as possible in sports, often participating in touch football games with his family and friends which might have led him to create one of his most famous quotes:

"We do not want our children to become a generation of spectators. Rather we want each of them to be a participant in the vigorous life."

John F. Kennedy – age 9, Dexter Academy

RICHARD NIXON

Richard Nixon was a reserve tackle for Whittier College in California, but his biggest football claim to fame came from a legendary story involving the Washington Redskins.

Known as Nixon's Play, the story claims that the Redskins coach George Allen, received a phone call from Nixon on the eve of their 1971 playoff game against the San Francisco 49ers.

Rumor has it that Coach Allen used the president's suggestion for a play against the 49ers, a play that lost the Redskins yardage and ultimately led them to lose the game.

RONALD REAGAN – "THE GIPPER"

Ronald Reagan was a lineman at Eureka College in Illinois, but his more well-known football connection is for portraying Notre Dame football great George Gipp in the 1940 film 'Knute Rockne, All American.'

Knute Rockne was portrayed by actor Pat O'Brien.

Reagan was given the nickname Gipper. Later in life he used the real George Gipp's famous deathbed plea to his coach "Just win one for the Gipper" as he was running for the presidency.

GERALD FORD

Gerald Ford was all-state at South High School in Grand Rapids, MI, and went on to become an MVP for the University of Michigan (even playing against the Chicago Bears as a member of the 1935 collegiate all-star team).

After turning down several pro football offers (including one from the Detriot Lions and one from the Green Bay Packers), Ford took a coaching position at Yale and applied to its law school.

Many of you readers may recall the early Saturday Night Live skits of Chevy Chase playing a bumbling President Ford. Actually the president was a gifted athlete and enjoyed skiing well into his sixties.

So what do we do now, It's halftime America.

Do we return to the offense, the defense, that got us here?

Do we throw it all out the door and join with the "economic offense" that is being practiced by the rest of the world? What is resulting is many desperate countries, throwing economic 'Hail Mary's", as they try to rescue themselves from the socialist pit into which they have dug themselves.

We have all been through different economic cycles in our lives and seen them in this country.

Sadly I did not think much about it all
You see I was cursed by being born in the USA. I have never known real hunger, or fear been unloved or forgotten like some.

Sometimes we have it too easy so we don't question, we don't take an interest, we don't stand up to be counted.

Think of the young quarterback that because of migration to the pros or graduation of his veteran offensive line, he suddenly finds himself in a huddle with all new lineman. Where are the senior guards and tackles that protected him, that lead the way on the QB sweep, that picked him up off the dirt and said cmon, "let's do this"

Well, they are gone and now he is on his own to find or deal with a different set of lineman. But he knows the plays, he knows that if all the players do their job, if they stick to what they have practiced, and everyone executes, they will be successful.

Now is the time
It's halftime and we have a whole new half ahead of us.

For the last 7-8 years we, as a country, have been playing a man down. The result of a stagnant economy, which has obviously hurt this country.

Ineffective, and at times feckless leadership, has caused a lowering of the collective bar.

We are getting accustomed to losing, accustom to a high unemployment rate and our economy is in a rut, we need an awakening to get back in the game.
A certain fear has enveloped our economy, causing stagnant growth and uncertainty. From what does this economic fear stem?

PETE CARROLL

Pete Carroll, highly successful college at USC and professional head coach of the Seattle Seahawks, put it this way.

"In my time as a coach, I've learned that possibly the greatest detractor from high performance is fear: fear that you are not prepared, fear that you are in over your head, fear that you are not worthy and ultimately, fear of failure.

If you can eliminate that fear, not through arrogance or just wishing difficulties away, but through hard work and preparation-you will put yourself in an incredibly powerful position to take on the challenges you face."

Let's strap that helmet back on, quit worrying and get back to business. But the government coaches have to get off the field and let us play.

"Let us play coach, let us play!"

Pete Carroll has been one of those rare big time coaches, that has been able to be successful at the college level and the pro level. Early on in his career he realized the need for a philosophy. This would be the game plan if you will, for succeeding in coaching no matter what school or team he was coaching.

Part of his philosophy follows.

(1)Create a Vision.

Pete decided that first he must create a vision, a game plan, a goal, that he would always have in mind. This vision would help him to make daily decisions, how to lead his life and reach the life goal if you will. This vision would be what he woke up to each day and went to bed thinking about each night.

As the coach himself stated" Personally I have learned that if you create a vision for yourself and stick with it, you can make amazing things happen in your life."

(2) Realizing that Vision and making it come true.

The coach knew that dreaming does not get you there. It is the hard work, discipline and continued effort to maintain that vision, that can make it all come true. As he said "The two go hand in hand. The moment you've created that vision, you're on your way, but it's the diligence with which you stick to that vision, that allows you to get there."

There are so many examples of the power of visioning. That power of creating a vision is so great that it can actually wok for you as well as against you"

(3) Visions become reality

Pete Carroll was one day visiting one of the more poor sections of Los Angeles, that of Watts.

He recalls asking a young man what his vision was for life. His matter of fact response was, "I'm either going to jail or I'm going to die."

Shocking as that was, the odds were that he was probably right, and they were increased by the fact that he was already laying out that plan in his own mind. If there ever was an example of negative affirmation, that was it. I could only respond by saying, "you're probably right, As long as that's the vision you hold for your life, that's likely what you're gonna get."

There is talk among many in this country that you would think we have forgotten the positive vision that has grown this country to be come the greatest country in the world. The talk is that the days of the American Dream and American exceptionalism are over, that there is a "New Normal" one where we are relegated by birth to our station in life, that 7-8% unemployment is going to be normal, that many of us just will not be able to "get ahead." Well clearly these folks have not heard of the power of a positive vision or have never heard Coach Pete Carroll explain his philosophy.

If we fixate on where we want to be, what we want to do and accomplish, and then put in the consistent effort, then there is no stopping us.

We as individuals have this vision, if only the nation's leaders would buy into it as well.

Pete's 3 Basic Rules

1) Always protect the team
2) No whining, No complaining, No excuses.
3) Be Early.

What great simple rules for a football team. There is no nebulous thought process involved here. These rules are as plain and easy to understand as they possibly could be. Now a naysayer here, may say,……..Nay. (By definition isn't that what a naysayer says? Honestly I have never met anyone that uses the word nay in everyday conversations, but, well, I digress here.)

A naysayer may say, "Well but I don't play football." Well, my friends even the simplest of minds can understand the correlation between these 3 rules, developed for competing in the game of Football and abiding by these rules when competing in the game of Life.

Coach Carroll once, was speaking with renowned San Francisco 49'ers coach Bill Walsh. Pete asked him about how he evaluates QB's. Coach Walsh said "All I'm looking for is a guy that can throw a catchable ball". "Joe Montana, didn't have the strongest arm but he could be relied upon to throw a catchable ball with near-total consistency"

For those who may have forgotten, Joe Montana was the quarterback for those great San Francisco 49 teams that dominated the NFL back in the 1980's. Indeed, Montana was not the biggest, fastest or strongest QB of the times, but he did what was most important for the team, he threw a "catchable ball."

We don't need the smartest most innovative leadership in our government, but we do need leaders that will create an environment, and in turn a sort of economic mentality, that makes growth or gives growth a high degree of success. In a sense we need someone that can throw an economic catchable ball.

This involves more of a "hands off", let 'em play" mentality. Government is not meant to be the driver of the economy any more than the head football coach is on the field throwing touchdown passes. It is the players, ie the citizens of this country, that given the chance to compete, without excessive rules or regulations, will make their own way, and achieve their own success.

In other words, get the coaches off the files and let the game begin. Who can throw a catchable ball?

Thinking of running for office Mr. Montana?

WHO GETS TO PLAY?

Who gets to play, those that work hard or those that feel they have the right to play.

Which works better?

"If you take a look at the work world today, no matter what profession, they're either looking for a person who is dedicated, hard-working, loyal and who is willing to make sacrifices for the company," said former DeMatha (Md.) Catholic High School head coach Bill McGregor. "They're also looking for someone who exhibits good character, leadership and class. I think they are all the intangibles that a young person can get from playing football."

Perhaps former Yale Sports Information Director Charles Loftus said it best in 1951: "A football player is a wonderful creature – you can criticize him, but you can't discourage him; you can defeat his team, but you can't make him quit.

"You can get him out of a game, but you can't get him out of football. ... He may not be an All-American, but he is an example of the American way. He is judged not for his race, nor for his religion, nor his social standing, or not for his finances but by the democratic yardstick of how well he blocks, tackles and sacrifices individual glory for the overall success of his teams."

We have become complacent in this country, with consistent unemployment, underemployment of millions that have given up their job search, miniscule quarterly growth, and high dependence on government assistance.

Politicians would like you to buy into the fact that these conditions are the "new norm" for this country. In their eyes we should be comfortable with this new environment, which I equate with second place.

MILTON FRIEDMAN said it best.

With a Nobel Prize in Economics, Milton Friedman knew a thing or two about the way an economy runs best. Despite the views of some, he stuck to his guns that capitalism is the driver of this nation, not socialism. Even when tested he stayed true to his principles.

In 1979 he was a guest on the "Phil Donahue Show." (Did Phil play baseball? I know he was a noted "lefty")

The exchange went like this:

Phil: When you see around the globe the mal-distribution of wealth, the desperate plight of millions of people in underdeveloped countries, when you see so many have-nots, when you see the greed and the concentration of power, did you ever have a moment of doubt about capitalism and whether greed is a good idea to run on?
Milton Friedman: Well first of all, tell me, is there some society you know that doesn't run on greed? You think Russia doesn't run on greed? You think China doesn't run on greed?
What is greed?
Of course none of US are greedy, it's the other fellow who is greedy. The world runs on individuals pursuing their separate interests.

The great achievements of civilization have not come from government bureaus. Einstein didn't construct his theory under order from a bureaucrat.

Henry Ford didn't revolutionize the auto industry that way. In the only cases in which the masses have escaped form the kind of grinding poverty you are talking about, the only cases in recorded history are where they have had capitalism and largely free trade. If you want to know where the masses are worse off, it's exactly in the kind of societies that depart form that. So that record of history is absolutely crystal clear that there is no alternative way, so far discovered, of improving the lot of the ordinary people that can hold a candle to the productive activities that are unleashed by a free enterprise system."

Phil Donohue: "But it seems to award not virtue as much as an ability to manipulate the system."

Milton Friedman: "And what does reward virtue?........I think you are taking a lot of things for granted. Just tell me where in the world you find these angels who are going to organize society for us"

Atta boy Milty, atta boy...................

TROPHIES FOR EVERYONE

Thanks in part, to the recent political leadership, we have become an "everyone gets trophies" society where we shun over achievers, lest they "offend" those that have not given the same effort. This author experienced this very result back in middle school football. I was a puny, (but slow) 7th grade lineman, I was selected, I like to think, because of my desire and hustle to receive a "letter" in football, something only a handful of 7th graders received, while playing for the "8th grade" team.

I was extremely proud, of this letter, especially since not everyone received one. Needless to say, I was disappointed later, when, under parental pressure, our head coach relented and "gave everyone letters (trophies)."

Is that what this greatest country in the world has been reduced to, do we do just do enough, to only have to just show up, so we can get a trophy? You hear of school systems that cancel scholastic and athletic awards dinners so as not to "offend" those underachievers" Well, it's this type of achievement/recognition that serve to motivate others into striving to become better at math, at speaking, the arts, athletics, whatever. If you have never been in second or third place, then you don't know the joy when one day you are the first place winner.

You have to have worked hard for something sometimes to really appreciate it.

One of the presidential wannabe's, is suggesting that the Federal government provide free, four year tuition at all state colleges and universities. Well, that term "Free" is a tricky concept, as someone has to pay for these tuitions, unless the university staff is working for free, as well. In reality it is not free, as the rest of the US taxpayers will be footing the bill, by funding yet another government program. Oh, but what's one more government program anyway, you ask. Well, would you ask a diabetic, "Oh, what damage can one more chocolate chip cookie do?"

Related to a football team, this program would be like a set up where only 8 of the 11 players have to do their job, while the other 3, enjoy the benefits, without really contributing.

"Oh, I don't think I'll block on this play, my foot hurts and that defensive tackle has not washed his socks recently."

In other words we have become way too comfortable with the economic mess in which we find our self, and so to add to the mess is of no consequence to some.

Real, effective, sincere leadership at the top, is what is needed, to create a positive atmosphere, in which the people of this country can compete, work and live in absence of fear.

Maybe it's time for a Knute Rockne speech and "Win one for the Gipper" and all that.

I like to refer to the great coach, Lou Holtz and his easy reference to always remember the word WIN, which is short for "What's Important Now"

Holtz used this easily remembered word to remind his players that what was past is just that. Forget what just happened and live in the moment, and do, What is Important Now.

So you missed a tackle on the last play, forget about it, What's Important Now? So you missed a block on the last play, What's Important Now? Don't look back, look forward.

This can just as easily be applied to the running of our country. For the last several years, this country has been in a state of confusion, in a never ending revolving door of indecision.

Let's forget about the high unemployment, the migration of jobs overseas, the poor foreign affairs showing, the current administration's push for class division, let's get back to "What is Important Now."

What is important now is to get back to the basics of opportunity for all and personal responsibility for all, that were the building blocks of this country. Let's get government back on the sidelines where it belongs, where coaches are supposed to reside, let the players on the field to make things happen.

Too much government, like too much coaching, suffocates the efforts of the players and the small business owners of this country. With a majority of the people of this country employed by small businesses, it is paramount that we reduce the regulatory stranglehold the federal government has on small business creation.

If the coaches,(government), will just get off the field and let the players play, this country, like a good football team, will come back.

Hopefully it will happen with the next Administration in Washington. Will it happen?

Well, to quote an un-named elementary school teacher of my boyhood pal, Mike Smith, "We shall see, what we shall see"

FOOTBALL IS BLUE
COLLAR AMERICA

As writer Steve Alic Sun put it,

Football is blue-collar America. It's working class, working together.

In this game – America's favorite sport – there is no "isolation play" that casts a team aside nor are there intentional walks to avoid an obstacle. In life, like football, the easy route is rarely an option.

Reflecting early America, football's fields are wide and open, but smart defenders – like challenging terrain – can hinder the most determined advancement attempt.

And great football teams are united, like the states we call home. We will make it back to greatness, if given the chance to play.

TONY DUNGY

Tony Dungy has played college football, coached in college, played professional football for a Super Bowl winner coached professional football, including a Super Bowl win with the Indianapolis Colts. He is a proponent, as are most good coaches of hard work and using the basics.

As he once said in a recent interview,
"Right now our society needs to get back to the fundamentals, those basic principles that allow us to succeed as men. We can be certain that there will always be obstacles along the way.

However, having these fundamentals to fall back on, will help us to overcome these obstacles. We are not only able to effect this change, but I think we need to.

The first thing you have to do to a team to change it from a loser to a winner is to create the belief that you can win.

The talent is there, we have to believe in ourselves again.

If you believe in yourselves, and begin to succeed, then this feeling catches on, particular with a team. You never know who may be watching you, so always do your best.

Tony Dungy relates a story from his days as a professional player, about the truth of this.

"When I came to the San Francisco 49's, after playing on a Super Bowl winning team, I noticed that one of my teammates had gotten into the drug culture of san Francisco, because he thought that's what athletes did. But because I had come from a Super Bowl winning team, and chose not to do drugs, it made him feel he didn't have to either. Years later, he told me that my example may have saved his life.

It was a lesson in role modeling I'll never forget."

Strap on that helmet and get back to work, display a positive attitude and greet everyone with a smile. It catches on.

People are watching you. Whose life will you positively impact today?

What can we do?

The third quarter is about to start, everyone is moving back to their seats,

The cheerleaders are warming up and the players are beginning to stream out of the locker rooms.

The second half kickoff will start soon.

The first half is history. We can determine the future of the country by what we do now.

So let's remember the word of Coach Lou Holtz, WIN.......... What's Important Now?

REFERENCES

P38-41
The Best Game Ever by Mark Bowden, Atlantic Monthly Press 2008

P55
Lou Holtz –Wining Every Day

P 19,20,22,24-26,42
The Real All Americans by Sally Jenkins, Doubleday, 2007

#77 The Gallopin Ghost, by Gary Andrew Poole

P28,30,33,4,52
The Gipper – Jack Cavanaugh

P 60-64 The Year that changed the Game-Jonathan Rand

P79-82 Be the Best Everyday – Pete Carroll

Printed in the United States
By Bookmasters